DUBAI

THE CITY AT A GLANC

CU00767092

Jumeirah Emirates Towers

One is a hotel, the other is an o
Linked by the city's most exclu
were the tallest buildings in D
years and one of its most fam
See p012 and p018

The Gate

The Arc de Triomphe of Dubai's business
heartland, touted as the missing link between
the bourses of Asia and Europe, is one of the
city's better bits of architecture.
See p074

Sheikh Zayed Road

The glittering glass ziggurats along the city's
main drag are the epitome of everything Dubai
wants to be – smart, efficient and business-
oriented. A convenient place to stay, or have
a coffee and perhaps dinner too.

Burj Dubai

Offices, apartments, the first Armani hotel.
Just how high the towering Burj Dubai will rise,
only Skidmore, Owings and Merrill know, but
it is already the tallest building in the world.
See p077

Shangri-La Hotel

Staff who remember your name, beds you
will not want to leave and breathtaking
master-of-the-universe views from the rooms
above the 40th floor. The Shangri-La may
not be heaven on earth, but it is definitely
a little piece of paradise.
See p023

INTRODUCTION
THE CHANGING FACE OF THE URBAN SCENE

Under its Middle Eastern veneer, Dubai is really Asian. Arabic is the national language and Islam is the official religion, but while you'll hear a *'salaam aleikum'* or two, Arabic is notably absent. As are the Arabs. Emiratis account for 15 per cent of the population; South Asians for 52 per cent; and a large proportion of the rest is made up of Iranians, Western expats and East Asians. In this city of others, English, Punjabi and Malayalam are all you need to survive.

Dubai embraces contradiction. A Gulf state with little oil of its own, it's an economic powerhouse. Uncomfortably close to the Iraqi nightmare and wedged between the hard-line Islamic republics of Saudi Arabia and Iran, it is an open and tolerant place. A city with significant global clout, its population is just 1.25 million.

It won't remain small for long. The official development plan has the population quadrupling and tourists reaching 15 million by 2010. People keep coming, and it isn't for a desert adventure. Dunes not already covered in asphalt are hidden under manicured lawns, lakes and parks. *Stepford Wives*-perfect, Dubai feels like a giant resort. The sheer speed of development is shocking. Entire neighbourhoods appear, apparently overnight. What the sheikh wants, the sheikh gets. An idea whose time has not yet come, a place with multiple identities, Dubai is a city in transition. Global hub, giant transit lounge, it's all about movement; and in a region locked in stasis, that alone makes it a marvel.

ESSENTIAL INFO
FACTS, FIGURES AND USEFUL ADDRESSES

TOURIST OFFICE
Visitor Information Bureau
Deira City Centre
T 294 8615
www.dubaitourism.ae

TRANSPORT
Car hire
Avis
T 343 7783
Hertz
T 224 5222
Dubai Transport
www.dubaitransport.gov.ae
Taxis
Cars Taxi
T 269 3344
Dubai Transport
T 208 0881

EMERGENCY SERVICES
Ambulance
T 998
Fire
T 997
Police
T 999
24-hour pharmacy
Binsina Pharmacy
Al Rigga Road
T 224 7650

EMBASSIES/CONSULATES
British Embassy
Al Seef Road
T 309 4444
www.britishembassy.gov.uk
US Consulate General
Dubai World Trade Centre
Sheikh Zayed Road
T 311 6000
dubai.usconsulate.gov

MONEY
American Express
2nd floor
Hermitage Building
Zabeel Road
T 336 5000
travel.americanexpress.com

POSTAL SERVICES
Post Office
Abu Hail Road, Deira
T 262 2222
Shipping
UPS
T 339 1939
www.ups.com

BOOKS
The Architecture of the United Arab Emirates by Salma Samar Damluji (Ithaca Press)
Dubai Architecture & Design by Architecture & Design Books (Daab)

WEBSITES
Art
www.thethirdline.com
www.artspace-dubai.com
Newspaper
www.khaleejtimes.com

COST OF LIVING
Taxi from DIA to Sheikh Zayed
€8.50
Cappuccino
€3.20
Packet of cigarettes
€1.50
Daily newspaper
€0.60
Bottle of champagne
€64

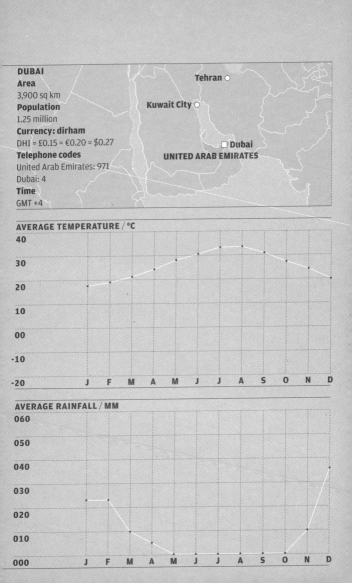

DUBAI
Area
3,900 sq km
Population
1.25 million
Currency: dirham
DH1 = £0.15 = €0.20 = $0.27
Telephone codes
United Arab Emirates: 971
Dubai: 4
Time
GMT +4

Tehran ○

Kuwait City ○

□ **Dubai**
UNITED ARAB EMIRATES

AVERAGE TEMPERATURE / °C

40											
30											
20											
10											
00											
-10											
-20	J	F	M	A	M	J	J	A	S	O	N	D

AVERAGE RAINFALL / MM

060											
050											
040											
030											
020											
010											
000	J	F	M	A	M	J	J	A	S	O	N	D

NEIGHBOURHOODS
THE AREAS YOU NEED TO KNOW AND WHY

To help you navigate the city, we've chosen the most interesting districts (see the map inside the back cover) and underlined featured venues in colour, according to their location (see below); those venues that are outside these areas are not coloured.

MARINA

Located between the shopping centres of Ibn Battuta and the Mall of the Emirates, and downwind from The Palm Jumeirah, Marina is one of Dubai's newest districts in the making. Pitched at creative types from the nearby Media and Internet Cities, as well as students thronging the overseas branches of the Western universities at Knowledge Village, it is envisaged as the cultural counterweight to the business hub rising behind Sheikh Zayed Road.

SHEIKH ZAYED

This glittering strip of glass ziggurats that lines the main highway to Abu Dhabi is everything brave new Dubai wants to be. Efficient and, above all, business-oriented, Sheikh Zayed may not be visible from space – but it can boast the world's tallest building, the Burj Dubai (see p077), which already dominates the skyline and is still to be completed. Pleasant cafés and many refined dining and nightlife options attract business visitors and expatriate residents.

DEIRA

Cramped, chaotic and crumbling, Deira could not be less like shiny new Dubai if it tried, which only makes it that much more interesting. Far from the skyscrapers and shopping malls, here tourists finally get a sense of being in the Middle East. Deira is a pedestrian's paradise – wander through narrow lanes, visit the city's first school, Al-Ahmadiya, or take a ride in a water taxi.

BUR DUBAI

The child of Dubai's first building boom in the 1960s, Bur Dubai looks a little rough around the edges these days. Blame an unforgiving climate, the abundance of 'old' buildings and the clash of styles. It's home to some great Indian restaurants, streets of Pakistani-owned electronics stores and a chunk of the city's architectural heritage.

JUMEIRAH

The low-rise mix of residential villas, cafés and malls lends Dubai's premier beachfront neighbourhood a more subdued air than the rest of the city. The maze of side streets hides boutiques, holistic treatment centres, day spas and home-furnishing outlets. And whether you fancy shopping, café-hopping, white-knuckle fun at Wild Wadi Water Park (T 348 4444, www.wildwadi.com) or a dip at the pristine public beach, Jumeirah has something for everyone.

CREEK

The biggest draws are the souks, Al Fahidi Fort (see p043), the Bastakiya district and the restored royal residences. But as the Creek winds through the bustle of the city towards the wildlife sanctuary in the marshlands of Jaddaf, it turns from waterway to urban leisure space. Two golf clubs and Creekside Park keep it green, while facilities at the under-construction Festival City (www.dubaifestivalcity.com) will add bars, clubs and live music venues to the restaurants that line the river.

LANDMARKS

THE SHAPE OF THE CITY SKYLINE

For a city that has made its reputation on superlatives – the tallest tower, the most expensive hotel – you'd expect Dubai to be awash with impressive buildings. But in reality, when it comes to finding structures that deserve to be called landmarks, that overgrown flagpole in Jumeirah aside, pickings are slim. At least for now.

Blame this on Dubai's twin weaknesses as a city: its relative youth and a development plan that has always placed making money before building anything memorable. As a consequence, city planners tore down almost everything historical years ago. Of course, there's always the Burj Al Arab (see p013), but after a while, you'll suspect the hotel's inescapable presence on T-shirts and postcards, and its transformation into stuffed toys, incense burners and gold-plated paperweights, proves that Dubai's most recognisable symbol is pretty much its only recognisable symbol.

Perhaps it is best to consider the landmark question on the macro, not the micro level. From its beginnings as a speck on the map – some former pearl-trading town where the less interesting airlines stopped to refuel on the way from Asia to Europe – Dubai has grown into a sprawling, rapidly metastasising city that, shades of Ozymandias aside, sees itself increasingly not just as a global hub but as *the* global hub. Forget individual buildings, Dubai's most impressive landmark just may be itself.

For full addresses, see Resources.

Dubai Marina
Just one of many new complexes under construction in the city, Dubai Marina, with its forest of cranes and scaffolding, is an ambitious scheme. Once finished, it will be the world's largest man-made marina and one of the most exclusive neighbourhoods in the city, comprising 200 high-rise buildings interspersed with villa-style residences, leisure areas and parklands.
Mina Al Seyahi, off Interchange 5, Sheikh Zayed Road, www.emaar.com

Jumeirah Emirates Towers

Near the World Trade Centre and right at the entrance to Sheikh Zayed Road, two equilateral glass and steel triangles rise 305m and 355m into the air. One is a hotel, the other an office building; and the two are linked by Dubai's most exclusive mall, The Boulevard. Set in 170,000 sq m of landscaping that includes a waterfall and garden, the NORR-designed towers dominate the otherwise low-rise financial district around them. The office tower, which was built in 2000, was the city's tallest finished building for seven years. The pair have been likened to pencil sharpeners and bottle openers, but they occupy a soft spot in many locals' hearts, being among the first of Dubai's buildings to gain international attention.
Sheikh Zayed Road, T 330 0000, www.jumeirahemiratestowers.com

Burj Al Arab

Okay, so the WS Atkins exterior rather resembles a giant Teflon beetle sat on its haunches, and the KCA International interior is so garishly overwrought that your first response may be laughter, but there is still something quite magnificent about your first sight of this hotel. Perhaps it's the way the building appears to catch the breeze when viewed from the side or perhaps it's because, at 321m, when built in 1999, it was the tallest hotel in the world. Once inside, your impression may not be as charitable. The 180m-high atrium is eye-popping, but 'signature experiences' like the submarine ride to the main restaurant are fairground, not fabulous, and the sheer hubris of having to pay a Dh37 entrance fee to set foot in the lobby is beyond irritating. *Off Jumeirah Beach Road, T 301 7777, www.burj-al-arab.com*

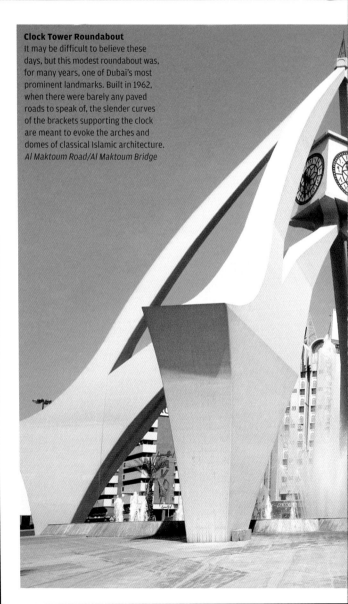

Clock Tower Roundabout
It may be difficult to believe these days, but this modest roundabout was, for many years, one of Dubai's most prominent landmarks. Built in 1962, when there were barely any paved roads to speak of, the slender curves of the brackets supporting the clock are meant to evoke the arches and domes of classical Islamic architecture.
Al Maktoum Road/Al Maktoum Bridge

HOTELS

WHERE TO STAY AND WHICH ROOMS TO BOOK

It is unfortunate that Dubai's most famous hotel is also its most garish. Fortunately, the self-styled 'seven star' Burj Al Arab (see po13), aka the hotel that taste forgot, is not representative. On the downside, Dubai doesn't really do budget accommodation, although some of the small business hotels clustered in Bur Dubai and Deira offer reasonable deals. The only genuine boutique hotels at the time of writing are XVA (see po20) and The Montgomerie (see po28).

On the plus side, competition between the hotels is fierce. All of them apparently offer some 'signature' product or treatment and all pride themselves on the warmth of their 'traditional Arab' hospitality, even if, in typical Dubai fashion, this is dispensed by Asians, not Arabs. The result is that, even at the lower end of the scale, service is courteous and generally very efficient.

During peak season, seemingly any time apart from summer, finding a room is a nightmare. With 10 million extra visitors a year expected by 2010, hotels feature heavily in Dubai's expansion, and all of the new 'cities' include at least a couple. By 2008, Dubai will boast a W and a Four Seasons, a second One&Only (see po32) and the first Armani hotel, in the Burj Dubai (see po77). Somewhat further off are Hydropolis, the much-hyped underwater hotel, and the Bawadi project, which will add 31 hotels to Dubai by 2014. Expect crystal towers and robot ninja guards.

For full addresses, see Resources.

Jumeirah Emirates Towers

Though it caused quite a splash when it opened, the Emirates Towers hotel and its rooms with their bold checked bedspreads and contrasting cushions, now appear a little dated, but then in breathless Dubai, where anything more than six months old is already an antiquity, that's a fate no hotel can avoid. Its location between the World Trade Centre and the Dubai International Financial Centre is the main draw for business travellers; female guests can book into the Chopard Ladies Floor, men can relax in the male spa (see p092) and visiting dignitaries should reserve the Royal Suite (overleaf). The lobby (above) is designed to impress the socks off clients; the view from Vu's Bar and Restaurant (see p061) should guarantee you seal the deal.
Sheikh Zayed Road, T 330 0000, www.jumeirahemiratestowers.com

Royal Suite, Emirates Towers

XVA

Housed in a beautifully renovated 70-year-old coral stone and adobe home in Bastakiya, XVA is unique. Not only does it offer guests the chance to experience an upscale version of life in a Dubai that actually no longer exists, but the tasteful way the nine rooms, such as the Deluxe (above), have been decorated with dark wood furniture, curtained bedsteads and mother-of-pearl inlaid furnishings by Lebanese designer Nada Debs, makes them a pleasure. Also an art gallery, café and boutique, the hotel is the work of American owner and long-time Dubai resident Mona Hauser, an erudite guide to all things Emirati. The breezy rooftop terrace is refreshing on hot summer nights, while the courtyard (right) is the place to relax in the winter. A book-filled 'TV room' is a cosy place to make new friends.
Al Fahidi roundabout, behind Basta Art Café, T 353 5383, www.xvagallery.com

Hilton Dubai Creek

This hotel underwent an overhaul in 2001, courtesy of Canadian architect Carlos Ott. It may be his deco aesthetic or perhaps it's the surfeit of black leather armchairs and chrome detailing found in the lobby, but there is a distinctly 1980s feel to the redesign. Something of a shock in a city addicted to all things faux-riental, the no-nonsense interior attracts a corporate clientele who doubtless appreciate a hotel as power(fully) dressed as they are. Rooms, such as the Executive Plus (above), are neat and spacious, the steely scheme softened by warm woods and crisp white linens on football field-sized beds. Book yourself into an Executive Plus room and relax in the jacuzzi or make for the bijou rooftop pool, which commands drop-dead views. *Baniyas Road, T 227 1111, www.hiltondubaicreek.com*

Shangri-La Hotel

Forty-three storeys tall, these two giant angular 'Ss' glow yellow in Dubai's dusty sky above the neon haze and sharp glass towers lining Sheikh Zayed Road. Basically, the Shangri-La is a business hotel with its eyes firmly on CEO-class travellers. Book yourself straight into one of the Horizon Club rooms on the 40th and 41st floors or the Presidential Suite (overleaf), where the panoramic views are enhanced by a regularly replenished supply of handmade chocolates, a capacious bed and a range of toiletries by Aigner. The Shangri-La is almost in a class of its own. Comprehensive amenities, seamless service and a heart-warming attention to detail ensure that, whatever your reason for visiting Dubai, your stay here will be one of the high points. *Sheikh Zayed Road, Satwa side, T 343 8888, www.shangri-la.com*

The Fairmont

The soaring atrium, with its acres of black marble, glass fountains, neon details and Cascades restaurant (right), makes such a bold impression that, on first sight, The Fairmont feels more like a lobby with a hotel attached. Still, it is not the décor that makes this hotel so popular with corporate travellers, but its comprehensive range of business services. Rooms are somewhat smaller than those available at other hotels in the same class, and while views are panoramic – over Sheikh Zayed or Jumeirah Beach and the Arabian Gulf – the huge windows, particularly in the corner rooms, can let in too much heat. Leisure facilities aren't ignored: aside from two pools, the hotel has one of Dubai's best spas (Willow Stream) and on Fridays serves one of the most over-booked champagne brunches in town.
Sheikh Zayed Road, Satwa side, T 332 5555, www.fairmont.com/dubai

The Montgomerie

Despite its name, The Montgomerie is more Thailand than Highlands. Overlooking a lake and surrounded by a 200-acre golf course, this small hotel is aimed squarely at travellers who bring their clubs wherever they go. From the outside, the place looks worryingly neoclassical, which only makes its pared-down, contemporary reception (right) and interior, with subtle earth tones and dramatic lighting, all the more of a pleasure. The 19 guest rooms, such as the Superior (above), in dark wood with white walls and mood lighting, have balconies overlooking the lake and, as they face away from the morning sun, are ideal for a private breakfast alfresco. Spend a day at the Angasana Spa, and when the sun goes down, relax with a cocktail by the pool or dine at Nineteen, the in-house Asian fusion restaurant.
Emirates Hills, T 390 5600,
www.themontgomerie.com

Grand Hyatt

The smooth curved exterior of the giant Grand Hyatt dominates Bur Dubai. Enter the very shiny lobby, with its gargantuan Swarovski chandeliers, four massive dhow hulls hanging from the ceiling and small river running through an indoor garden that is just a few branches short of being a fully fledged rainforest, and it's clear this hotel was built to impress. It is essentially a resort away from the beach. There are four pools, a spa, full gym facilities and squash and tennis courts, all set in 37 acres of landscaped grounds. Rooms are spacious and comfortable, but the décor is blandly international. Odd-numbered rooms come with spectacular floor-to-ceiling views of the palm-fringed Creek, the airport and the glass towers of Deira. *Oud Metha Road, T 317 1234, www.dubai.grand.hyatt.com*

Grosvenor House

From the welcome drink and chilled towel that greets you on arrival in the lobby (above), to the selection of desserts and appetisers laid out in your room, the Grosvenor prides itself on being a class act. It's located on the edge of the city on the seafront side of the Marina district, and as new developments are finished, Dubai's centre of gravity will shift the hotel's way. Looking all Manhattan in the 1930s from the outside, its blue neon exterior lighting belies a sophisticated interior. The Asian feel is carried through to the rooms, styled with dark wood and cream upholstery. Beds big enough for a team of bodyguards, toiletries by Bulgari and seafront rooms overlooking the ever-rising Palm create an almost Zen ambience.
West Marina Beach, T 399 8888,
www.grosvenorhouse-dubai.com

One&Only Royal Mirage

The Royal Mirage could be the beachside equivalent of the Park Hyatt (overleaf). Like its inner-city sister, it is all about romance and understated elegance, and aims to be a destination in its own right. Decorated in a pan-Arabian style, rooms, such as the Deluxe (right), are stuffed with every amenity known to Homo Hotelicus. Choose the butler-serviced Garden Villa at the Residence and Spa for some extra pampering, whose rooms are a hop, skip and jump from the warm waters of the Gulf, and where guests have access to a separate dining area and pool. Throughout the hotel, service seems to anticipate your every need, and you may wonder if staff actually have psychic abilities. Spend the morning on the beach, the afternoon at the spa and the evening eating by the pool, and you may never want to leave.
Al Sufouh Road, T 399 9999,
www.royalmiragedubai.com

Park Hyatt

Nestled between the two halves of Dubai Creek Golf & Yacht Club (see p094), the Hyatt's whitewashed Moorish exterior, with its discreet zellij tiles, sparkling blue cupolas and tropical greenery, gives only the barest hint of the glamour within. Public spaces, such as the Tranquility Garden (left), are understated and hyper-elegant, and the modern, light-filled rooms are pitch perfect, while the Royal Suite (above) is suitably decadent. Open-plan bathrooms stocked with products by Blaise Mautin mean couples should either know one another intimately or be ready to gain that knowledge. The waterfront bar, intimate courtyard pool, fine dining and romantic Amara spa (see p089) make the Hyatt a one-stop destination.
Dubai Creek Golf & Yacht Club, T 602 1234, www.dubai.park.hyatt.com

Kempinski Hotel

As it is attached to the third largest indoor ski resort in the world (see p044) and the region's biggest shopping centre, Mall of the Emirates (T 409 9000), you might wonder how the Kempinski, which opened in 2006, will hold its own. Decorated along an alpine theme, the 'cool' lobby (above), with its white marble and cascading water features, is integrated into the mall via the cosy Aspen Café. Accommodation includes a clutch of three-floor ski chalets, two of which overlook the slopes, the bedroom level faces the Gulf. The hotel's rococo exterior hides a playful, modern interior. Rooms are snug, lavishly minimal but well appointed, and come with lots of high-tech gewgaws. This hotel is enormously popular with the oversized sunglasses crowd. *Mall of the Emirates, Sheikh Zayed Road, T 341 0000, www.kempinski-dubai.com*

Al Maha Desert Resort & Spa

A cross between a tented city and a luxury safari lodge, the Maha is deep inside a nature reserve outside Dubai proper. As you arrive, the first living creatures you encounter are the long-horned oryx that wander the grounds. Each guest is assigned their own South African ranger, who is there to answer questions about birdlife and breeding habits, to arrange jaunts into the desert and, of course, to have the champagne and strawberries ready at sunset. You can lounge by the pool at the spa or in private at the small pool outside your air-conditioned tent. Scattered along the ridge of a massive dune, tents, such as the Bedouin Suite (above), are so well screened that a skinny dip is possible, and highly recommended. *Between Dubai and Al Ain, T 303 4222, www.al-maha.com*

Bedouin Suites, Al Maha

24 HOURS

SEE THE BEST OF THE CITY IN JUST ONE DAY

It makes sense in a city that prides itself on offering everyone everything they could possibly want, that your perfect Dubai day should run the gamut from natural to artificial, luxury to cheap and cheerful, and give you the chance to sample a little history, to shop, and to enjoy food from the four corners of the world.

Start out early with some piping hot *mankoushe* for breakfast at the packed Lebanese fast-food chain Zaatar w Zeit (opposite). Then head to the urban wildlife sanctuary at Ras Al Khor (T 206 4240) at the end of Dubai Creek. After some flamingo spotting, head to Deira and rummage around the souks in search of fluorescent Syrian pants and pseudo-Persian rugs from China (see p042). From there, ride an *abra* (water taxi) from the wharf at Al Ras across to Bastakiya, to explore the neighbourhood's galleries and the oldest building in the city, the Al Fahidi Fort (see p043).

As the afternoon winds down, take a taxi to Blue Sail (Al Seef Road, T 397 9730), then a speedboat onto the open seas for a sunset cruise, cocktail in hand. Ask to be dropped off near Dubai Marina (see p010) and grab a cab to Ski Dubai (see p044) in the Mall of the Emirates. You've had sun and sea, now experience downhill fun. Then head back to Deira, and the Hong Kong Restaurant (see p046) for dim sum. Varied, multicultural and slightly surreal, your day has covered a lot of ground in a short time. Dubai, in a nutshell. *For full addresses, see Resources.*

08.30 Zaatar w Zeit

A genuine outpost of Beirut in Dubai, this Lebanese chain is the perfect place to fortify yourself at the start of a long day. There are baked goods, including *fatayer* (pastry pockets filled with spinach, meat or cheese), and sizzling hotpots (try the cheese, ham and egg combo), but ZwZ, as it is known, is famed for its *manakeesh*, usually referred to as Lebanese pizza. The description is accurate, but doesn't do it justice as *mankoushe* (the singular of *manakeesh*) comes in savoury or sweet varieties and can be ordered as *furn* (a thick base) or *saj* (lighter and crispier). Try the *zaatar jibneh saj* (thyme and cheese) or a *lahme beajine* (minced meat and tomato), and finish up with a *chocolat moze saj* (banana and chocolate). Absolute heaven. *Sheikh Zayed Road, near the Shangri-La Hotel, T 329 0400*

11.30 Souks

Instead of buying your souvenirs in an air-conditioned mall, indulge your senses with a trip to the souks in Creek. It's true, the experience will be more sweaty, you'll have to haggle and opening hours are less convenient (generally 8am or 9am-1pm and 4pm-9pm or 10pm, closed Fridays), but for their bustle alone, the markets are more interesting than the malls. Creek's souks are close to each other and each specialises in different goods: gold, food, antiques or spices. Wares tend to be a little more mixed, and you'll have to dig through a lot of tat, often from India, China or Iran, but your chances of finding something you haven't seen before are higher here than elsewhere, particularly at the more upmarket boutiques like Majlis Gallery (above, T 353 6233).
Between Baniyas and Al Mussallah Roads

14.30 Al Fahidi Fort

Stop for lunch in the quiet courtyard
of the Basta Art Café (T 353 5071). Order
a sandwich and a large salad – the Souk,
with its mix of couscous, chicken and
cashews, is particularly satisfying. Linger
over a mocktail or two, before exploring
the galleries and boutiques of Bastakiya.
Try Majlis Gallery (opposite) for traditional
offerings and watercolours, or XVA (see
p020) for something more contemporary.

Then bolster your cultural credentials with
a trip to the nearby Al Fahidi Fort (above).
Built in 1799, the fort has been transformed
into the fairly uninspiring Dubai Museum,
which relies a little heavily on waxworks,
but it is well worth a quick visit to admire
the traditional architecture up close.
Al Fahidi Street, T 353 1862

19.30 Ski Dubai
A trip to Dubai, the self-described Las Vegas of the Middle East, is not complete without indulging in at least one tacky experience. So remind yourself that you are in one of the most surreal cities in the Gulf and head to the 400m slope at Ski Dubai (open until 11pm weekdays; midnight at the weekends). In the evening, the slopes are empty of squealing first-timers.
Mall of the Emirates, Sheikh Zayed Road, T 409 4000, www.skidxb.com

23.30 Hong Kong Restaurant

You know you are in the right place for a spot of *yum cha* when the clients are all Chinese, the menu is photocopied and the décor – think paper lanterns, bamboo plants and black and white furniture – is funky, not feng shui. A taste of Hong Kong, and definitely Kowloon rather than the Island, this simple restaurant specialises in the delicate, mostly steamed Cantonese delicacies, which are better known outside the Chinese-speaking world as dim sum, or 'heart's delight'. Try the *cha siu bao* (slightly sweet pork buns), *ha gau* (shrimp dumplings) or the lotus leaf wrap. Not to be missed are the pan-fried beef *siu mai* (dumplings again), Chinese custard tarts and deep-fried sesame balls. Wash your supper down with pots of tea; oolong leaves are particularly good at cutting through the starch and the oil.
Sun & Sand Hotel, Rigga Al Buteen Road, T 223 9000, www.sunsandhotel.com

URBAN LIFE
CAFÉS, RESTAURANTS, BARS AND NIGHTCLUBS

Nightlife in Dubai is indistinguishable from nightlife in Europe or the US. Comedy clubs feature acts fresh from London and dance clubs host DJs who were in Barcelona the night before and are on their way back to Berlin. It's all a bit, well, same-ish.

The biggest immediate difference, apart from the abundance of Arabian-themed interiors, is that strict controls on alcohol mean most good restaurants and nearly all the bars and clubs are in (five-star) hotels. This adds glamour to going out, but a hotel is not the most exciting place to spend an evening. So, when you want to escape the lobby scene, try Chandelier (Sheikh Zayed Road, T 366 3606), a white, angular, Lebanese restaurant with a loud, colourful crowd, or sample the glitzy seaside vibe at Sho Cho (Dubai Marine Beach Resort & Spa, Jumeirah Beach Road, T 346 1111).

For something more raw, visit the water-pipe restaurants and cafés of Deira and Karama. Most don't serve alcohol, and so attract a non-Western crowd. Slip into Egyptian shisha heaven at Fatafeet (Al Seef Road, T 397 9222) or try one of the curry houses in Karama. In Dubai, you find most cuisines from Italian to Tibetan, but it is difficult to find decent local food outside a private home. So if you fancy *gerger*, *dango* or a plate of *ouzi*, you need to hit the tourist traps. Try Kan Zaman (next to Dubai Heritage Village, T 393 9913) and Al Areesh (Al Boom Tourist Village, T 324 3000).
For full addresses, see Resources.

Traiteur

Offering modern European cuisine in a striking setting vaguely reminiscent of a mid-century wooden auditorium, Traiteur, in the Park Hyatt hotel (see p034), is split between an upper level, complete with wine bar and outdoor terrace area, and a lower level, better for summer or daytime dining. Open-plan and airy, a sculptural enclosure that looks like a giant rib cage offers a little privacy on the lower level, but diners in search of something more intimate should book their own dining room or check out the sublimely chilly Cave Privée, the well-stocked wine cellar adjacent to the restaurant. The menu favours meats, but a variety of salad and provençale-style fish dishes will delight anyone with a yen for something lighter. *Park Hyatt, Dubai Creek Golf & Yacht Club, T 602 1234, www.dubai.park.hyatt.com*

Verre

Gordon Ramsay's first restaurant
outside the UK, Verre opened in 2003.
Thanks to head chef Jason Whitelock's
skill at interpreting Ramsay's brief,
you will need to book a week to 10 days
ahead (dinner only, closed Saturdays).
The menu is as sparse as the interior
and, as befits a port, favours seafood.
*Hilton Dubai Creek, Baniyas Road,
T 212 7550, www.hiltondubaicreek.com*

Lime Tree

It will probably remind you a little of the wholefood cafés you used to eat in when you were a student, but the Lime Tree has several appealing features. First, it offers one of the rare opportunities in the city to eat good food outside a hotel or a shopping mall. Second, it serves excellent, if simple, dishes. And third, your body will thank you for giving it a break from all the spices, seafood and steak you've been feeding it of late. Huge but interesting salads, quiches, tarts and frittatas and mountainous desserts are best washed down with a lime mint soda. The lavish breakfasts are popular with the 'baby on board' crowd and the place is usually packed with newspaper-toting expatriates, but don't let that deter you. It's a colourful treat.
Beach Road, T 349 8498

The Roof Top

Looking out over The Palm Jumeirah, The Roof Top has an atmosphere that is second to none. Hypnotic music, a mix of lounge and chilled-out Arabic, and the low, cushion-covered divans combine to create a lethally serene atmosphere. Relax, kick your shoes off and stretch out. Order a cocktail or two and pretend you are a pasha for a day. Though not necessarily the place for making new friends – the crowd is usually beautiful, but cliquey – this is an intimate venue for getting to know friends better. *Arabian Court, One&Only Royal Mirage, Al Sufouh Road, T 399 9999, www.royalmiragedubai.com*

Indego
Although it features Hindu gods and assorted Indian tchotchkes, the interior at Indego, the work of Vineet Bhatia, owner of Rasoi near London's Sloane Square, is uncluttered, leaving the focus on the food. Smoky tandoori prawns and mustard chicken come recommended. *Grosvenor House, West Marina Beach, T 399 8888, www.grosvenorhouse-dubai.com*

Sezzam

With its dramatic modern design, view of the artificial ski slope (see p044) and multiple kitchens, Sezzam makes a strong first impression. There is everything from Asian and Middle Eastern to European dishes on offer, all presented according to the way they are prepared rather than by ethnic origin. Fancy a pizza? Go to the Bake area. After some dim sum? Try Steam. Nothing tempting you yet? Try the Flame kitchen; it serves tandoori meats, barbecues and grilled fish. Unfortunately, Sezzam doesn't know what it wants to be. It touts itself as a fast-food and fine dining eaterie and lounge bar, but by trying to be everything, it ends up as nothing, which overshadows the fact that the quality here is very good – for a food court. Come for a quick lunch and you won't be disappointed. *Mall of the Emirates, Sheikh Zayed Road, T 341 3600, www.sezzam.com*

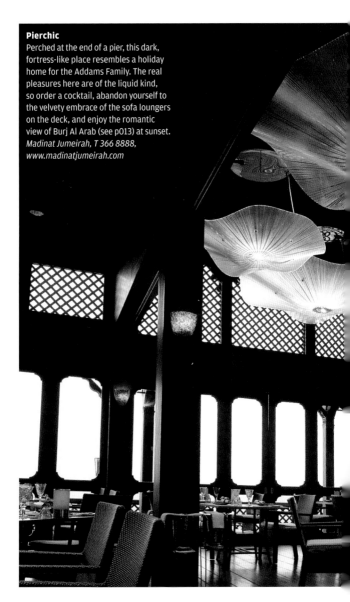

Pierchic
Perched at the end of a pier, this dark,
fortress-like place resembles a holiday
home for the Addams Family. The real
pleasures here are of the liquid kind,
so order a cocktail, abandon yourself to
the velvety embrace of the sofa loungers
on the deck, and enjoy the romantic
view of Burj Al Arab (see p013) at sunset.
Madinat Jumeirah, T 366 8888,
www.madinatjumeirah.com

Kasbar

Opulent and lavishly decorated, this Moroccan-themed extravaganza is so popular with Dubai's resident and visiting glitterati that it could be subtitled 'dance with supermodels'. Despite this, Kasbar can be a fun place to hang out, and not only to indulge in some celebrity spotting. Far less up for it than neighbouring Trilogy (see p068), Kasbar plays Arabic and lounge music, not techno or nosebleed, and the clientele is older and infinitely wealthier. The fact that this bar is inside the lovely One&Only Royal Mirage hotel (see p032) explains the first factor, and a quick glance at the price list explains the latter. Leave your credit card at home. *One&Only Royal Mirage, T 399 9999, www.royalmiragedubai.com*

Vu's Bar

Perhaps it's the sloping glass roof and atmospheric lighting, or maybe it's the 51st-floor setting, but the view here, of a glittering cityscape, is enough to make anyone feel like a Master of the Universe. Another draw is the selection of fine wines and cocktails, including a martini capable of turning your head if the view doesn't do it for you. Of course, that's one reason Vu's is popular with the corporate crowd. Another reason is the food served in the restaurant (overleaf). The menu has a Pacific Rim spin, evident in the delicately herbed fish and meat dishes. It's the work of chef Jason Viles, late of Mint in Sydney. Whether for dinner or a drink, Vu's is one of Dubai's more elevated experiences. *Jumeirah Emirates Towers, Sheikh Zayed Road, T 319 8088, www.jumeirahemiratestowers.com*

The One

Located in a store best described as a cross between The Pier and The Conran Shop, this dramatic all-black café, with its glass-bead curtains, so-called 'Louis Farouk' ornate furniture and Philippe Starck knock-offs, is particularly popular, you won't be surprised to discover, with male interior decorators and their female friends. The One is about as close as Dubai gets to a gay café and the menu is fabulous too: Earl Grey teacake, Pacific Rim Marie Rose sandwiches (papaya, avocado, heart of palm and spicy tofu), wild mushroom and puy lentil haggis, Thai baked Alaska and more varieties of tea than you cared to believe could exist. Survey the clientele, who are most certainly surveying you, or alternatively, just enjoy the view of Jumeirah Mosque next door.
1 Jumeirah Beach Road, T 345 6687

Almaz by Momo

Mourad Mazouz's Middle Eastern outpost is a riot of zellij tiles, intriguing stencil designs, dark glitter ceiling panels and brightly coloured terrazzo tiles from Lebanon. The menu is modern Moroccan, light and flavoursome, but most dishes will be familiar to anyone who has eaten Moroccan before. For those who haven't, the young, attractive, multicultural staff are more than happy to advise. Eat in the main room (above), choose the more secluded confines of the tent-like yellow dining area, or savour a selection of snacks as you smoke a water pipe in the Shisha Lounge (overleaf). Almaz is alcohol-free and attracts local customers as a result. Some of the mocktails are so convincing, you may get a buzz anyway.
Level 2, Harvey Nichols, Mall of the Emirates, T 409 8877, www.altayer.com

Trilogy

Take several hundred sweaty girls in
tight dresses, add a truckload of excited
Egyptian men, dot with a sprinkling
of club kids and creative types, add
a roster of top-name Euro DJs, and you
have Trilogy, Dubai's most popular
club. Try to navigate your way to the
roof, which is used for VIP events.
*Madinat Jumeirah, T 366 8888,
www.trilogy.ae*

INSIDER'S GUIDE

ZAYAN GHANDOUR, FASHION BOUTIQUE OWNER

Born and raised in Beirut, Zayan Ghandour has made Dubai her home for the last six years. She is co-owner of fashion and lifestyle store S*uce (pronounced Sauce), described in American *Vogue* as the 'boutique that bounced with style'. She loves to promote the old souks in downtown Deira, for their great reject stores and haberdasheries, and her favourite bargain market is Souk Nayef (next to the spice and gold souks), a treasure trove of appliqués, vintage buttons and lace ribbons, which she buys to embroider on to her own collection of T-shirts (www.zayan.com).

Her favourite chill-out spot is the XVA gallery-cum-boutique hotel and café (see po20); for its delicious fresh-mint lemonade and interesting mix of people, and for fast food, nothing beats the Al Reef Lebanese Bakery (Al Wasl Road, facing Safa Park, T 396 1980), where innovations include fava-bean pizza.

For the best one-off party dresses, Ghandour favours designs by the Dubai-based couturier Essa and she finishes off her look with handmade earrings and accessories by Turkish designer Fusun, all available from S*uce (The Village Mall, Jumeirah Road, T 344 7270). At weekends, she likes to smoke rose-flavoured shisha at the Zyara Café (Union Tower, Sheikh Zayed Road, T 343 5454). For dinner, it's always Teatro (Towers Rotana Hotel, Sheikh Zayed Road, T 343 8000), which serves a wide range of dishes from Indian to Italian. *For full addresses, see Resources.*

ARCHITOUR
A GUIDE TO DUBAI'S ICONIC BUILDINGS

Billy Idol once said that he was an idol because he called himself one. Dubai has apparently taken a leaf from the singer's book and labours under the belief that by labelling every new building 'iconic', however undeservedly, the description will stick.

Even up to a decade ago, you could get away with such tricks. Architecturally, the Gulf hadn't progressed much beyond its coral stone and adobe vernacular, so when the oil money started to flow in the 1960s, if you threw up a tall building you could claim the cutting edge. That is no longer the case. Inspired by Dubai's success, and flush thanks to an oil boom, Abu Dhabi, Qatar, Bahrain and Kuwait appear to have decided that their future cachet should, in part, be based on starchitecture. Dubai has a lot of tall buildings, but few do more than remind you of better ones elsewhere.

It's a sign of maturity that Dubai has finally understood that, in terms of architecture at least, quantity is not quality. Zaha Hadid's much-delayed project, dubbed the 'Dancing Towers', should now be complete by 2008, as should Lord Foster's One Central Park. It could be that the city will embrace architecture with the same zeal it showed for construction. If not, in about a decade or so, when its neighbours come into their own, Dubai's star will wane, and if there were anything the city that hype built could not bear, it would be to surrender the limelight to its sisters.

For full addresses, see Resources.

National Bank of Dubai

This 1998 building is the work of Canadian Carlos Ott, the architect behind the reviled Opéra de la Bastille in Paris, and was arguably Dubai's first deliberately iconic building. It is certainly Ott's best work, at least in Dubai. His much-lauded Hilton Creek revamp is cold in comparison, and his current project, 2008's B2B Tower in Business Bay, is also uninspiring. But this 125m-tall tower, with its sail-shaped glass façade, is meant to evoke the dhows that ply the Creek, and the tension in the arc of its mirrored surface suggests the building is about to sail across the city. It is especially attractive just before dusk, when it catches the light of the setting sun and sends it shimmering across the water, and after dark, when the lights from the offices within turn it into a giant electronic display.

Baniyas Road, T 310 0101, www.nbd.com

The Gate

Yes, you have seen something similar before – in Paris. Got it yet? No? Well then picture a cartouche of romantic neoclassical sculpture on either column, replace the square arch with a round one and…you could almost be on the Champs-Élysées. The gateway to Dubai's new business hub shows that tasteful reinterpretation is not a bad thing.
Dubai International Financial Centre

Traditional home, Bastakiya

It's a bit of a cheat, because this is not a recommendation for a single building. But, with some of the last remaining examples of Dubai's pre-oil vernacular, the Bastakiya district's narrow lanes give a sense of how the city lived before it discovered concrete, air conditioning and mirrored glass. Houses here have been rebuilt to varying degrees after years of neglect. The majority are now shops, restaurants or galleries, but a handful have once again become private homes. Some are more lavish than others, and Philately House (T 353 8383) is especially recommended, but in terms of structure, they are quite similar, with thick clay walls, rooftop wind towers and central courtyards. The cubist aesthetic feels radically more modern than most of the arabesque skyscrapers going up elsewhere.

Burj Dubai

From its wide, flat base, this Skidmore, Owings and Merrill-designed Y-shaped tower spirals upwards, sections falling away, until in the last few hundred metres the slender central core emerges. At the time of publication, the exact height of the world's tallest building, to be finished in 2008, was a secret, with estimates from 705m to more than 900m. The design is derived from the geometrics of a desert flower, with each segment conceived of as a petal. Mindful of its location, this mixed-use hotel, residential and office building alludes to Islamic architectural motifs, such as domes and archways, in a largely symbolic manner. Technical tricks include a double-glass skin, designed to help reduce the absorption of heat. History rising, as the billboard says.
www.burjdubai.com

Capricorn Tower

This slender 185m-tall residential and office building on the Dubai International Finance Centre side of the Sheikh Zayed Road is easy to overlook. The work of Chilean architect Borja Huidobro, it is a simple affair, given to discreet touches of architectural luxury. The six-storey atrium, for example, might be acceptable in a hotel, but in a commercial building in Dubai, unbuilt space is anathema, unless it can be used to hang advertising or double as a warehouse. Here, the atrium does neither, but serves only to dramatise the entrance and lighten the tower by raising it, as if on piloti, above the ground. Seductive in its simplicity, and proof that less really is more.
Sheikh Zayed Road

SHOPPING

THE BEST RETAIL THERAPY AND WHAT TO BUY

Consumerism is a national sport in Dubai, and when temperatures regularly exceed 30°C, who'd want to be kicking a football around anyway? The city has some of the best shopping in the Gulf region. The sheer number of brands, all tax-free, explains the appeal to visitors from India, Iran and the neighbouring states. For most others, there's not a lot on offer. In a city where everything comes from somewhere else, there isn't much that your average Londoner, Singaporean or Tokyoite couldn't find at home.

But it isn't all bad. The souks are fun and, while they don't have the cachet of the malls and lack the gravitas of the souks of Aleppo in Syria and Shiraz in Iran, they are atmospheric places to wander around. Dubai is short on boutiques and small businesses, but it is still a young city. Art galleries like The Third Line (Al Quoz 3, T 341 1367) and B21 (Al Quoz 3, T 340 3965) are creating a regional art hub, and designers are slowly arriving. Try Kube (Showroom 5, opposite Enoc House, T 335 7657) for Indian fashion.

What Dubai does offer is custom-made. Bring a photo of what you want, find material at the Textiles Souk (near Al Fahidi Street) and haggle hard at tailors like Kachins (Meena Bazar, Cosmos Lane, T 352 1386) or Dream Girl (Al Fahidi Street, T 352 1841). For jewellery, try the Gold Souk (Old Baladiya Street) or the upscale Gold and Diamond Park (Sheikh Zayed Road, T 347 8235).

For full addresses, see Resources.

Shiffa

When Lamees Hamdan couldn't find any anti-stretchmark oil she trusted when she was carrying her first child, she decided to make her own. Of course, as a trained dermatologist, Dr Hamdan did have an advantage, but the range she created, which includes bath oils, skin creams and scented candles, is the work of someone who is passionate about taking care of much more than just the surface. Organic, preservative-free and hypo-allergenic, the luxurious, richly scented products, which are sold under the Shiffa brand (the word means 'healing' in Arabic), are made from local ingredients wherever possible, which is no mean feat in import-it-all Dubai.
Harvey Nichols, Mall of the Emirates, Sheikh Zayed Road, T 269 0887, www.shiffa.com

Five Green
Tired of malls? Try Five Green, a place
where consumerism meets culture, all
neatly packaged in tasteful surroundings.
Local architectural practice DXB-LAB
teamed up with London's KoderCraft to
create this bijou boutique, which sells
streetwear collections and redeems its
immortal soul with art events.
*Garden Home, Oud Metha Road,
T 336 4100, www.fivegreen.com*

Villa Moda

An outpost of Sheikh Majed Al-Sabah's burgeoning Villa Moda fashion empire, which has become the Gulf byword for luxury, this high-concept store stocks fashion from the likes of Stella McCartney, Prada, Chloé, Marni, Collette Dinnigan and Comme des Garçons, and boasts more than 50 men's and women's brands. If that were not enough enticement, this is one of Dubai's most interesting shops in terms of design. Bold and futuristic, with more than a touch of the 1960s about it, the interior is the work of Jean-Philippe Evrot. *The Boulevard, Jumeirah Emirates Towers, Sheikh Zayed Road, T 330 4555*

Gallery One

Is it a store with a gallery attached or a gallery with a store attached? Either way, you will probably find something you'll want to take home. Ignore the forgettable photos of ye olde Dubai and stock shots of endless skyscrapers and dhows. Instead, concentrate on two areas – the gallery and the huge collection of photographic prints taken from the archive at Beirut's Arab Image Foundation. The latter is a fascinating mix of pan-Arab kitsch, mostly advertisements, still shots from Egyptian films and political propaganda, but also intimate portraits culled from private collections and defunct photo studios from Cairo to Casablanca. All chart the evolution of attitudes in the Arab world, and there are a few surprises.
Shop 138, Souk Madinat Jumeirah,
T 368 6055, www.g-1.com

Ajmal Eternal

It's no coincidence that when the Three Wise Men came bearing gifts, they brought frankincense and myrrh. Without the Arabs, the temples of Egypt and Rome, not to mention the churches of Europe, would have smelled entirely differently. Ajmal, one of the Gulf region's largest retailers of essential oils and perfumes, has given this ages-old commodity a modern twist. It sells powerful, musky, woody and floral oils alongside sinuously simple perfume bottles made of Murano glass. At Eternal, the oils are of a higher quality than those sold at ordinary Ajmal branches, and the oud chips – pieces of perfumed wood from India burned on special occasions – are similarly superior. *The Boulevard, Jumeirah Emirates Towers, Sheikh Zayed Road, T 330 0600, www.ajmaleternal.com*

SPORTS AND SPAS

WORK OUT, CHILL OUT OR JUST WATCH

Doha may well have pipped Dubai to the sporting post by creating a national sport academy (ASPIRE) to train the Arab athletes of the future, and by winning the rights to host the 2006 Asian Games, but Dubai isn't about to allow Qatar to take all the glory. This is why the biggest development project in town, the multibillion-dollar 278 sq km behemoth Dubailand (www.dubailand.ae) will transform Dubai's existing and already extensive sporting facilities.

Chief among these elements are an artificial ski resort, at least five new multi-use stadiums, a Formula One-standard racetrack, a championship golf course and the world's largest water park. It will take the better part of a decade to complete. Until then, there is plenty to amuse. For the armchair athlete, the highlights are offshore power boating in December and, in March, the highest-stakes horse racing event in the world, the Dubai World Cup.

The brave can get into a scrum with the Dubai International Rugby Sevens (www.rugby7.com), fence with an Arab champion at the Metropolitan Hotel (Sheikh Zayed Road, T 343 0000), play at being Robin Hood at the Dubai Archers Club (Dubai Country Club, off Ras Al Khor Road, T 333 1155), go scuba-diving on the reefs not destroyed by the building of The Palms (Al Boom Diving, Al Wasi Road, T 342 2993; or Scubatec, Shop 15, Karama Sana Building, T 334 8988) or shoosh downhill at Ski Dubai (see p044). *For full addresses, see Resources.*

Amara

A trip to Amara spa in the Park Hyatt hotel (see p034) is hard work. Kick off with a foot and hand wash, followed by a Dead Sea-salt body scrub infused with spices, then rinse off in the outdoor rain shower in your private courtyard. Relax on the garden sofa, enjoying your peppermint tea, dried apricots and crunchy almonds, then return for your aromatherapy and Swedish massage session, where you are alternately pounded and slathered with oils that leave your skin soft for days. Return to the rain shower, then collapse on the couch, or move to the central courtyard, where, in the evening, the oil lights in the pool and the star-filled sky above will relieve any residual tension. Arise remade and ready to fall into bed.
Park Hyatt, Dubai Creek Golf & Yacht Club, T 602 1234, www.dubai.park.hyatt.com

Club Mina
With one of the nicest beaches in Dubai, a kilometre of carefully swept sand backing onto palm-tree-dotted grounds, complete with outdoor table tennis, Club Mina's other facilities only increase its appeal. These include three large pools, a gym, tennis courts and a marina.
Le Meridien Mina Seyahi Beach Resort, Jumeirah Beach, Al Sufouh Road, T 318 1421, www.lemeridien-minaseyahi.com

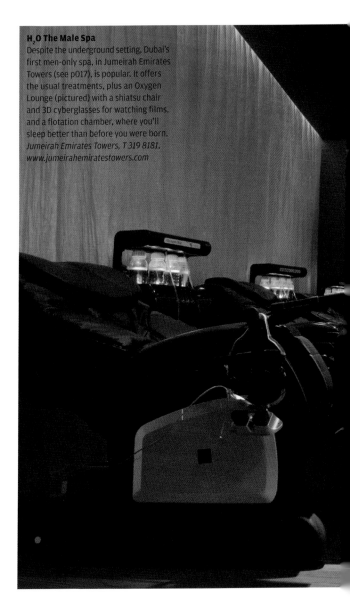

H₂O The Male Spa
Despite the underground setting, Dubai's
first men-only spa, in Jumeirah Emirates
Towers (see p017), is popular. It offers
the usual treatments, plus an Oxygen
Lounge (pictured) with a shiatsu chair
and 3D cyberglasses for watching films,
and a flotation chamber, where you'll
sleep better than before you were born.
Jumeirah Emirates Towers, T 319 8181,
www.jumeirahemiratestowers.com

Dubai Creek Golf & Yacht Club
Of all Dubai's golf courses, the Creek is definitely the most conveniently located. Right in the middle of the city, between the business district of Garhoud and the Creek, it has a sixth-hole tee on stilts, 10m out into the river. The 18-hole par 71 championship-standard course was given a complete overhaul in 2004 by Danish PGA golfer Thomas Björn, and a floodlit nine-hole course can be played until 10pm, making it possible to get in a game after a hard day of meetings or pounding the malls. If that isn't enough, consider booking into the on-site hotel, the Park Hyatt (see p034). With an academy run by four full-time PGA instructors ready to perfect your swing, this two-time host to the Dubai Desert Classic was rated as one of the top courses in the world in 2005 by UK magazine *Golf World*.
Opposite Deira City Centre, Al Garhoud Road, T 295 6000, www.dubaigolf.com

ESCAPES

WHERE TO GO IF YOU WANT TO LEAVE TOWN

So much conspicuous consumption eventually wearies the most ardent capitalist, and when thoughts turn to escape, Dubai offers four options: the desert, the sea, another emirate or a flight out. The last is the only option for a genuine change of scenery. As for neighbouring cities, it's only in terms of development and amenities that the six other emirates differ. That said, a trip to Sharjah (see p100), Ras Al Khaimah, or even the capital, Abu Dhabi (opposite) will give visitors a better sense of regional context.

In the winter, the desert can be a lot of fun. Visit the historic fort at Hatta (see p098); the abandoned village of Wadi Hayl; the prehistoric archaeological remains at Al Bithnah; the hot springs at Ain Al Gamour; go sand-skiing or race a Land Cruiser up towering dunes (Budget, Jumeirah Emirates Towers, T 319 8733). A calmer option is a 4x4 desert tour. After a juddering trip up a dry valley and a camel farm visit, a typical day ends with a barbecue at a Bedouin 'encampment', complete with a belly dancer.

For something more edifying, try the nature reserve in the mangrove forest at Khor Kalba, or spot endangered species on Sir Bani Yas island, near Abu Dhabi. Then there is the sea, which offers scuba-diving and deep-sea fishing, as well as waterskiing, sailing, and all manner of watersports. Try Scubatec (see p088) and Dubai Water Sports Association (Dubai Creek, T 324 1031). *For full addresses, see Resources.*

Abu Dhabi

Abu Dhabi is the largest and richest of the seven emirates that make up the UAE. It has the best beaches, the nicest coastline, the most oil. But while Dubai, a 90-minute car ride away, has long since changed unalterably, Abu Dhabi is still just about recognisable as the modest fishing port it was when oil was first found in 1958. That is all about to change. Frank Gehry is to break ground on a 30,000 sq m Guggenheim Museum on Saadiyat Island, while the emirate has become the fastest-growing international market for global couture. Fortunately, the state's bold future has already arrived in the colossal shape of the Emirates Palace (above). You will struggle to find a hotel anywhere in the world with a more beautiful private beach. *West Corniche Road, T 02 690 9000, www.emiratespalace.com*

Hatta Heritage Village

The 115km trip to Hatta is a lovely excuse to see some desert. After a visit to this heritage village, with its fortified houses and 200-year-old mosque, head on down the road to spend an afternoon of pure pleasure in the icy pools that dot the shaded valley past Buraimi. Break your return journey with a sundowner by the pool at the Hatta Fort Hotel (T 852 3211). *T 852 1374, www.dubaitourism.ae*

Sharjah

The emirate of Sharjah doesn't look a bit like its big sister, Dubai. Admittedly, your first sight is of a shopping mall, but soon you'll notice the high-rises aren't as high, the hotels aren't as many-starred and the restaurants are more sober. There is an emphasis on Islamic values (no alcohol, nightclubs, short sleeves or miniskirts), Arabic, not English, is the language of choice, and in place of massive development projects and glitzy malls, there are 15 of the 21 museums in the UAE and 'traditional' bazaars. The archaeological (T 06 566 5466), Islamic (T 06 553 334) and art (T 06 568 8222) museums are all worth a visit. The contemporary exhibit at the Art Museum shows work produced at Sharjah's international plastic arts biennial (www.sharjahbiennial.org).

Musandam

A large part of the Gulf region's oil passes through the 60km-wide strait separating Iran from the Arabian Peninsula, which is one reason why, until fairly recently, visitors were rarely allowed here. Another is because Musandam belongs to Oman, and relations between it and the UAE have not always been close. These days, however, getting there is easy. This is a good thing because, with its plunging cliffs, secluded bays and rugged scenery, and topography that has earned it the epithet the 'Arabian fjords', Musandam is extraordinarily beautiful and remote. You can arrange for a driver and a boat tour through tour operators in Dubai. Arabian Adventures (T 303 4888) and Khasab Travel and Tours (T 266 9950) are good bets. Spend a night at the basic but charming Khasab Hotel (T 968 2 673 0271).

NOTES

SKETCHES AND MEMOS

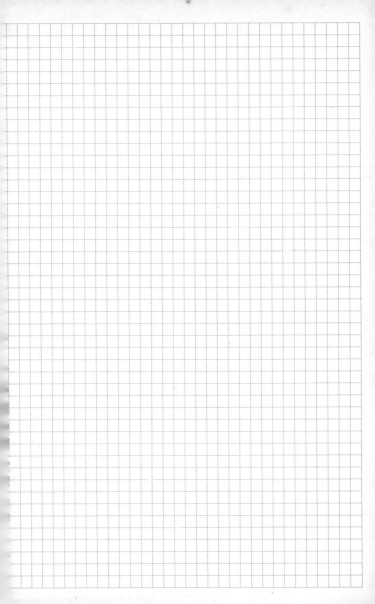

RESOURCES
CITY GUIDE DIRECTORY

A

Ajmal Eternal 086
The Boulevard
Jumeirah Emirates Towers
Sheikh Zayed Road
T 330 0600
www.ajmaleternal.com

Al Areesh 048
Al Boom Tourist Village
Beside Al Garhoud Bridge
T 324 3000

Al Boom Diving 088
Al Wasi Road
T 342 2993
www.alboomdiving.com

Al Fahidi Fort 043
Al Fahidi Street
T 353 1862

Almaz by Momo 065
Level 2
Harvey Nichols
Mall of the Emirates
Sheikh Zayed Road
T 409 8877
www.altayer.com

Al Reef Lebanese Bakery 070
Al Wasl Road
Facing Safa Park
T 396 1980

Amara 089
Park Hyatt
Dubai Creek Golf & Yacht Club
T 602 1234
www.dubai.park.hyatt.com

Arabian Adventures 102
4th floor
Emirates Holiday Building
Sheikh Zayed Road
T 303 4888
www.arabian-adventures.com

Archaeological Museum 100
Sheikh Zayed Road/
Al-Hizam Al-Akhdar Road
Sharjah
T 06 566 5466
www.archaeology.gov.ae

B

Basta Art Café 043
Al Fahidi roundabout
T 353 5071

Blue Sail 040
Al Seef Road
Opposite British Embassy
T 397 9730

B21 080
Al Quoz 3
T 340 3965

Budget 096
Jumeirah Emirates Towers
Sheikh Zayed Road
T 319 8733
www.budget.com

Burj Al Arab 013
Off Jumeirah Beach Road
T 301 7777
www.burj-al-arab.com

C

Capricorn Tower 078
Sheikh Zayed Road

Chandelier 048
Inside Marina Walk
Sheikh Zayed Road
T 366 3606

Clock Tower Roundabout 014
Al Maktoum Road/Al Maktoum Bridge

HOTELS
ADDRESSES AND ROOM RATES

Al Maha Desert Resort & Spa 037
Room rates:
Bedouin Suite, from DH3,495
Between Dubai and Al Ain
T 303 4222
www.al-maha.com
The Fairmont 026
Room rates:
double, DH1,799
Sheikh Zayed Road
Satwa side
T 332 5555
www.fairmont.com/dubai
Grand Hyatt 030
Room rates:
double, DH900
Oud Metha Road
T 317 1234
www.dubai.grand.hyatt.com
Grosvenor House 031
Room rates:
double, DH2,250
West Marina Beach
T 399 8888
www.grosvenorhouse-dubai.com
Hilton Dubai Creek 022
Room rates:
double, from DH600;
Executive Plus, from DH1,000
Baniyas Road
T 227 1111
www.hiltondubaicreek.com

Jumeirah Emirates Towers 017
Room rates:
double, DH2,700;
Royal Suite, DH9,000
Sheikh Zayed Road
T 330 0000
www.jumeirahemiratestowers.com
Kempinski Hotel 036
Room rates:
double, DH1,704
Mall of the Emirates
Sheikh Zayed Road
T 341 0000
www.kempinski-dubai.com
The Montgomerie 028
Room rates:
double, from DH888;
Superior Room, from DH888;
suites, from DH1,130
Emirates Hills
T 390 5600
www.themontgomerie.com
One&Only Royal Mirage 032
Room rates:
double, DH1,990;
Deluxe, DH1,990;
Garden Villa, DH14,550
Al Sufouh Road
T 399 9999
www.royalmiragedubai.com
Park Hyatt 034
Room rates:
double, DH1,600;
Royal Suite, from DH10,650
Dubai Creek Golf & Yacht Club
Opposite Deira City Centre
Al Garhoud Road
T 602 1234
www.dubai.park.hyatt.com

Shangri-La Hotel 023
Room rates:
double, DH1,000;
Horizon Club room,
DH980-DH2,950;
Presidential Suite,
DH12,000-DH20,000
Sheikh Zayed Road
Satwa side
T 343 8888
www.shangri-la.com

XVA 020
Room rates:
double, DH650;
Deluxe, DH750
Al Fahidi roundabout
Behind Basta Art Café
T 353 5383
www.xvagallery.com

WALLPAPER* CITY GUIDES

Editorial Director
Richard Cook

Art Director
Loran Stosskopf
City Editor
Warren Singh-Bartlett
Project Editor
Rachael Moloney
Executive
Managing Editor
Jessica Firmin

Chief Designer
Ben Blossom
Designer
Ingvild Sandal

Map Illustrator
Russell Bell

Photography Editor
Christopher Lands
Photography Assistant
Jasmine Labeau

Chief Sub-Editor
Jeremy Case
Sub-Editor
Vicky McGinlay
Assistant Sub-Editor
Milly Nolan

Intern
Sylvie Subba

Wallpaper* Group
Editor-in-Chief
Jeremy Langmead
Creative Director
Tony Chambers
Publishing Director
Fiona Dent

Contributors
Paul Barnes
Jeroen Bergmans
Alan Fletcher
Sara Henrichs
David McKendrick
Claudia Perin
Meirion Pritchard
James Reid
Ellie Stathaki

PHAIDON

Phaidon Press Limited
Regent's Wharf
All Saints Street
London N1 9PA

Phaidon Press Inc
180 Varick Street
New York, NY 10014
www.phaidon.com

First published 2007
© 2007 Phaidon
Press Limited

ISBN 978 0 7148 4721 4

A CIP Catalogue record
for this book is available
from the British Library.

All prices are correct at
time of going to press,
but are subject to change.

Printed in China

PHOTOGRAPHERS

Jon Challicom
Zayan Ghandour, p071

Gulf Images
Dubai city view, inside
front cover

Roger Moukarzel
Almaz by Momo,
p065, pp066-067

Mai Nordahn
Clock Tower Roundabout,
pp014-015
XVA, p020, p021
The Montgomerie, p028,
p029
Zaatar w Zeit, p041
Majlis Gallery, p042
Al Fahidi Fort, p043
Ski Dubai, pp044-045
Hong Kong Restaurant,
pp046-047
Traiteur, p049
Verre, pp050-051
Lime Tree, p052
Indego, pp054-055
Sezzam, pp056-057
Pierchic, pp058-059
The One, p064
Trilogy, pp068-069
National Bank of Dubai,
p073
The Gate, pp074-075
Traditional home,
Bastakiya, p076
Burj Dubai, p077

Capricorn Tower,
pp078-079
Shiffa, p081
Five Green, pp082-083
Gallery One, p085
Ajmal Eternal, pp086-087
Amara, p089
Club Mina, pp090-091
Dubai Creek Golf & Yacht
Club, pp094-095
Hatta Heritage Village,
pp098-099
Musandam, pp102-103

Jonathan de Villiers
Dubai Marina, pp010-011
Burj Al Arab, p013

DUBAI
A COLOUR-CODED GUIDE TO THE HOT 'HOODS

MARINA
One of the city's newest neighbourhoods will be a cultural centre aimed at creative types

SHEIKH ZAYED
The world's tallest building dominates this business district full of nightlife options

DEIRA
Chaotic and crumbling, the old town provides a rare but charming taste of the Middle East

BUR DUBAI
This 1960s suburb is a hotchpotch of architectural styles and myriad Indian restaurants

JUMEIRAH
Boutiques, cafés and spas line the side streets of this low-rise beachside playground

CREEK
An expanse of freshwater that's home to a wildlife sanctuary, two golf clubs and a park

For a full description of each neighbourhood,
including the places you really must not miss, see the Introduction